A Purnell Book

MAKE A MODEL

VICTORIAN HOUSE

Devised and illustrated by

Sue Shields

First published in Great Britain in 1983 for Marks and Spencer plc
New edition published in 1987 by Macdonald & Co (Publishers) Ltd
Greater London House
Hampstead Road
London NW1 7QX
A Pergamon Press plc company

Reprinted 1988
ISBN 0 361 07837 4

Printed in Great Britain by Purnell Book Production Ltd A member of BPCC plc

Life in Victorian Times

A Time of Change

Victoria's reign lasted longer than that of any other British monarch—sixty-four years, from 1837 until 1901. During that time life was desperately hard for a lot of people, despite the improvements introduced by social reformers. Among these were laws which forbade small children to work in coal mines or as chimney sweeps and in 1870, around the time that our house was built, a new education law was passed which said that all children between the ages of five and thirteen must go to school. This did not go down well with all parents, because not only did they have to pay a little towards this education, but the poorer ones needed the few pence that the children could otherwise earn.

Houses like this house were being built in ever-increasing quantities in all Britain's cities. There were much humbler dwellings appearing, too—the tiny workers' cottages which housed the many factory workers, drawn from the country to the towns, where they could earn more money in the new factories that were springing up everywhere.

Queen Victoria's reign was a time of great progress, when inventions were patented which were to change the course of life all over the world. In the middle of all the hardship of the ordinary people, brilliant ideas were being tried out which were, eventually, to provide better living conditions for millions.

The coming of the railways spread an iron network around the country, enabling people to travel more freely than ever before. When Victoria came to the throne in 1837, there were already 200 miles of railway. Sixty years later there were over 20,000 miles of railway—and they were being used not only to carry people from place to place, but also to transport goods, letters and parcels. This made postage cheaper, and encouraged people to write letters.

Sewing machines, typewriters, gas cookers—many things in use today were first introduced in Victorian times. Maybe the most revolutionary of all is the motor car—or is it the telephone?

The Great Exhibition

In 1851 a Great Exhibition took place in Hyde Park. It was masterminded by Prince Albert, Queen Victoria's husband, as a celebration of all the best of Victorian industry. A Crystal Palace was erected to house the Exhibition. It was designed by the architect, Joseph Paxton and made out of plate glass and iron girders. The Exhibition was a tremendous success. Inside the great, glass building were examples of everything that represented British life

The early days of the motor car—Daimler in his self-moving carriage

—furniture, clothing, model cottages—all the latest in industrial design. Over six million people visited it, and the profit made from it was used to buy the land for the Natural History Museum and the Victoria and Albert Museum.

Health in Victorian Times

With so many people living closely together in towns, disease spread fast. The water that people drank was often filthy and epidemics of such diseases as cholera spread into rich homes as well as poor. It was 1875 before a law was passed which forced the authorities to clean up the sewers and drains, and to purify all drinking water.

As the century wore on, an interest in health developed. This was partly due to the introduction of anaesthetics for operations by James Simpson, and antiseptics for lessening the risk of infection by Joseph Lister. Those caring for sick people were also shown the importance of cleanliness. Florence Nightingale, too, was more than just a good nurse. She started a training school for other nurses, and published papers which helped people to see that fresh air was good for them.

Victorian bathing dress and bathing machine

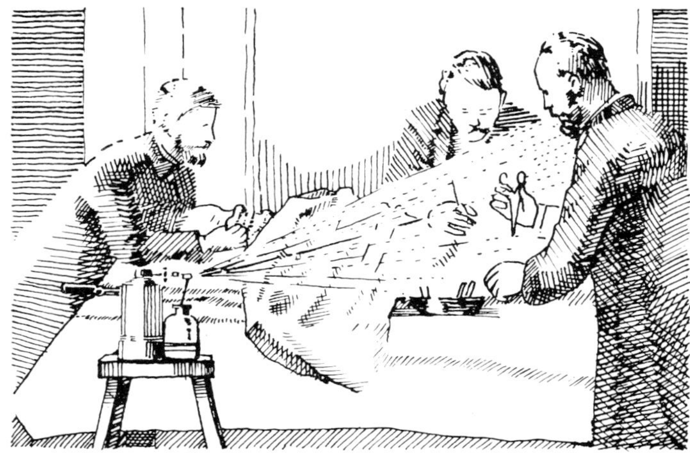

Joseph Lister and his disinfectant spray

If you were sick and rich, there was enough money to pay for medical treatment, a luxury the poor people often had to do without. When you felt better, you might go to a seaside resort to recover in the bracing coastal air. As a result of this, seaside places became popular.

Seaside Holidays

The railways had made it easy and cheap for people to reach the coast, so many people began to spend time beside the sea for fun as well as for their health. Tiny seaside towns blossomed into the resorts we know today with rows of hotels and guest-houses. People enjoyed strolling along the newly-built promenades and piers as well as having fun on the beaches.

Not that you might think it much fun if you were made to behave at the seaside as a Victorian child did! Rarely were they allowed to take off their shoes and socks, and they were well dressed-up too, in layers of clothes which would be unthinkable today.

Towards the end of the century bathing became popular. But there was no undressing on the beach! If you wanted to bathe, you hired a bathing-hut, which was wheeled down into the water. A door opened into the sea, and you came out very quickly, slipped into the water without anyone seeing you, and climbed back in again afterwards to change. Not that the Victorian bathing costumes were at all revealing—they extended to the knees, and often had elbow-length sleeves as well!

Life in the Victorian World

Picture yourself standing inside this Victorian house when it was brand new. You are looking out of the window—but at what sort of world?

If you had been rich enough to enjoy such luxury you would have known very little about the world outside. You would have grown up protected from the poverty that many people suffered, right on your own doorstep.

You would not have to go to school. A tutor or governess would be employed for you and your brothers and sisters. The boys would later be sent off to boarding school, but the girls would remain at home to learn about household management and ladylike things such as sewing, piano-playing and painting, in order that they would make good wives in the future.

Your father would have owned this house, and he would have earned at least £20 per week. That may not seem very much in today's terms, but in 1870 it was really quite a lot of money. Ordinary working men earned around ten shillings a week—that's 50 pence in today's decimal currency. A miner might earn three times that, but an ordinary working girl could slave away from dawn to dusk in a factory for four shillings, or 20 pence, a week.

Very likely there would be a maid in your house who might be only about thirteen. She would be fed by your family and live in the house. Her wages would probably be sent home to her mother, except for a few pence—because her 20 pence could make the difference between life and starvation to a large family of younger brothers and sisters.

Your father would work hard too, for it was considered to be one's duty and privilege to work hard. No one allowed his children to be idle either, so even as a rich child you would not be pampered or allowed too much of your own way.

Whatever happened, you would feel secure in the love of your family. If it were a typical Victorian one, there would be plenty of brothers and sisters to provide all the company you would need. Queen Victoria herself had nine children, and the nation modelled itself on her.

In the Home

The day began for the family's servants long before any of the master's family awoke. At some early hour of the morning, even before the sun was up, the maids would be hard at work, cleaning rooms, emptying grates and lighting fires so that all would be ready for the family when they began their day. Shoes had to be cleaned, steps polished, floors swept; in some houses there was such attention to detail that even the daily newspaper had to be ironed before the master read it!

These days, when our knives and forks are made of stainless steel and our saucepans may have non-stick linings, it is hard to imagine what it must have been like before such inventions. Cutlery had to be thoroughly polished by the maids in Victorian times, and there were no easy surfaces to help the washing-up. When anyone in the master's family wished to have a bath, someone else had to rush upstairs with steaming jugs of water. Even switching on a light, without electricity, involved lighting a gas lamp, or an oil one, which had to be kept trimmed so that it didn't smoke.

Family prayers, at which the servants stood behind the family, would take place before breakfast and were led by the master of the house. Religion was a part of everyday life. Grace was said before meals and children always said their prayers at bedtime.

Small children would spend most of their time in the nursery, attended by a nanny and maybe a nurse-maid, too. Older children might see a bit more of their parents; they might be taught to read and count by their mothers, who sometimes also attended nursery meals to teach table manners to their young ones. Only when they reached the stage of governesses and tutors would the children be allowed to share meals with their parents in the dining-room . . . and they were expected to keep quiet throughout the meal, too!

It might have been a relief to return to the nursery once more and relax a little. All the toys and books

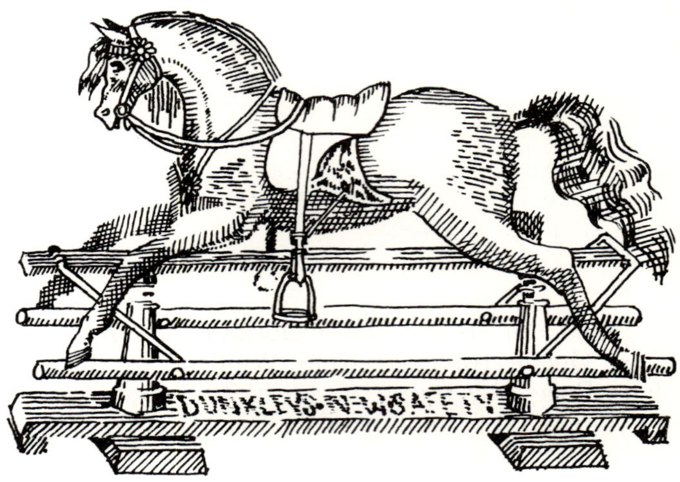

A Victorian rocking horse

were kept there, and many have survived the years so that we know just what Victorian children played with.

There would have been toy theatres made of paper, sometimes already coloured and sold for two-pence or plain black and white, to colour yourself, for half the price.

Jigsaws were popular, too. Parents encouraged the use of any toy which seemed to be educational, so these often showed maps and other such useful things.

A fascinating toy was the zoetrope, in which many

A zoetrope

pictures, each one slightly different from the one before, revolved inside a drum. You peered at these pictures through slits in the side, and as the drum spun round, the people or animals in the pictures appeared to be moving. This must have seemed like sheer magic to a child who had never seen a cartoon film or watched a television set.

There were clockwork toys, rocking horses and dolls, just as there are today. And many nurseries would have a doll's house, too, so those far-off Victorian children would be doing the same as you, when you play with this house.

The Golden Jubilee

When Queen Victoria came to the throne on June 20th, 1837, she was only just eighteen years old. Fifty years later she was not at first in favour of any special celebrations in honour of her Golden Jubilee. She had rheumatism, and didn't look forward to all the 'hustle and bustle' that such an event would entail. But when the Prince of Wales presented her with a special inkstand, decorated with a crown, to commemorate the Jubilee, she began to get interested, and soon preparations were in hand for a national celebration.

June 20th, 1887, was a glorious summer's day. The Queen travelled from Windsor to Buckingham Palace by train for most of the way, continuing through cheering crowds on the drive from Paddington to the Palace. Royalty from all over the world banqueted with her at luncheon and dinner. The following day there was a thanksgiving service in Westminster Abbey; but she refused to dress up in her robes of state and a crown, and insisted on wearing a bonnet! All the ladies in the procession had to wear bonnets too, for who could be crowned while the Queen wore a bonnet?

The next day there was a huge party for the poor people, in Hyde Park. Thirty thousand schoolchildren received a Jubilee mug in honour of the occasion. And the Queen herself, who had not received any wedding presents from the people when she had married Prince Albert in 1840, now found to her amazement that gifts were pouring in from all corners of her land, in gratitude for the prosperity and status that her realm now enjoyed.

When you have made the Victorian House in the centre of the book you can have fun acting the play in the second part of the book. It is set on the day of Queen Victoria's Golden Jubilee.

Why not try writing one of your own, too!

A MODEL VICTORIAN HOUSE

The house in this book is a typical Victorian Villa (the Victorians often called their houses villas), although most houses would have had more rooms to accommodate large families and servants. We have really "chopped a house in half" so that you can get inside! As you walk through the front door you come face to face with Queen Victoria herself—not in person, of course! The wallpaper with the Queen's portrait was specially made for the Golden Jubilee in 1887.

Let's walk down the hall to the kitchen. Cook was in charge of the kitchen with its iron range on which all meals were cooked. The ovens in the range were good for making bread, too. This one is fuelled by logs as you can see.

Next to the kitchen is the dining room where the family ate their meals. Notice the ornamented wallpaper and the fussy curtains. Victorian rooms were highly decorated and often rather dark.

From the dining room you can walk into the light, airy conservatory—a popular feature as the Victorians were fond of plants.

The drawing room was usually on the first floor, and this was where the family would entertain guests. Note the exotic wallpaper which was produced in 1875 to commemorate the Prince of Wales' visit to India.

Opposite the drawing room is Father and Mother's bedroom. All the rooms have fireplaces. There was no central heating, so in winter there would be fires in the bedrooms, too.

Let's go up to the top floor. On the left is the girls' bedroom with a beautiful wallpaper called Sleeping Beauty. The alphabet pictures on the wall are actual copies of ones you could buy in Victorian times.

On the other side of the landing is the maid's room. Most families had several maids living in.

Bathing in front of the fire

You may wonder where the bathroom is. Bathrooms were not common until the very end of the nineteenth century, so chamber pots were used—and maids had to run up and down from the kitchen to the bedrooms with jugs of hot water for washing.

The house may look luxurious, but Victorian life wasn't as comfortable as life today with all our modern conveniences.

Making the Victorian House

You will need:
Sharp scissors or a craft knife
A ruler
A tube of transparent glue
A table knife
Paper clips (optional, but useful for holding glued pieces in place until dry)

General Instructions

Cutting
Cut out along the thick black lines.

Slots
Where there are two thick black lines close together cut between them to make a slot.

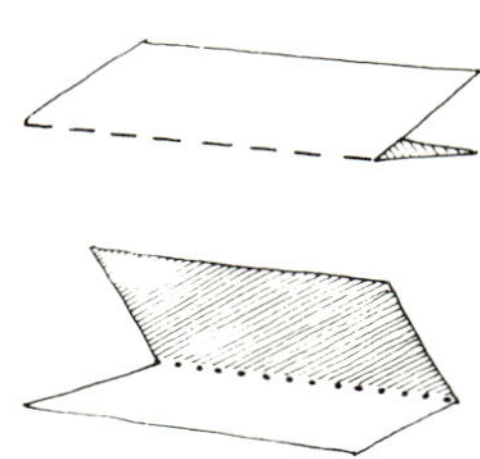

Folding
If a line is dotted, fold card towards you.
If a line is broken, fold line away from you.
Before folding, place a ruler on the line, and run a table knife down the ruler to score the card.
This will make sure the card folds cleanly, and in the right place.

SHEET A **Walls of House**

1. Cut out the pieces and fold as indicated.
2. Glue tab A1 to space A1.

SHEET B **Inside Walls, Stairs and Roof**

1. Cut out the pieces, cut wall slots as shown under doors. Fold as indicated.
2. Fold the roof before cutting the slots out. Put the roof to one side.
3. Open out the inside walls. Glue tab B1 of the stairs to space B1 on wall. Glue tab B2 to space B2.

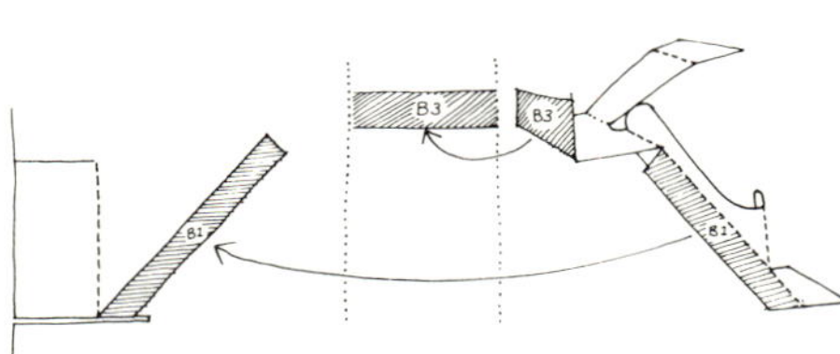

4. Fold stair-wall so that you can then glue tab B3 to space B3 and tab B4 to space B4.
5. Glue the back of the stair-wall to the wall of the house as indicated.

SHEET C **Top floor, First Floor, Base and Garden**

1. Cut out pieces and fold as indicated.
2. Deal with the top floor first. Put glue on spaces C1, C2, C3, C4, slide the floor into position, so that each tab meets its space.

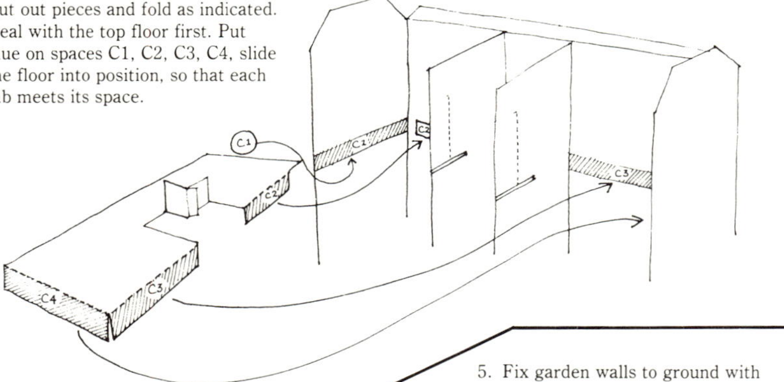

3. Repeat this process with the first floor. Glue C5, C6, C7 and C8 and slide in to meet their spaces.
4. Position tops of both stairs, glue down carpet at top and bottom of stairs, and glue top-floor bannister to back of chest of drawers.
5. Glue house to base matching tabs to spaces.

SHEET D **Verandah and Conservatory, Ceiling and Chimneys**

1. Cut out and fold pieces.
2. Form conservatory by gluing tab D1 to space D1.
3. Form verandah by gluing area (marked D2) inside balustrade, pinch balustrade together until glue holds. Complete folding.
4. Glue this section to the house with tabs D3, D4, D5 and D6, then glue it to the ground with tabs D7, D8, D9, D10, D11, D12 and D13.
5. Fix garden walls to ground with tabs D14 and D15.
   Fix to house with tabs D16 and D17, and to front wall with tabs D18 and D19.
6. Take ceiling and chimney section, glue to house with tabs D20 and D21.
7. Take roof and open flat. Fold in flat sides of chimney and thread through roof slots.
8. Press down top of roof enough to release sides of chimney, then pull up centre fold of roof, so that tabs B7 and B8 correspond to their spaces, then glue.

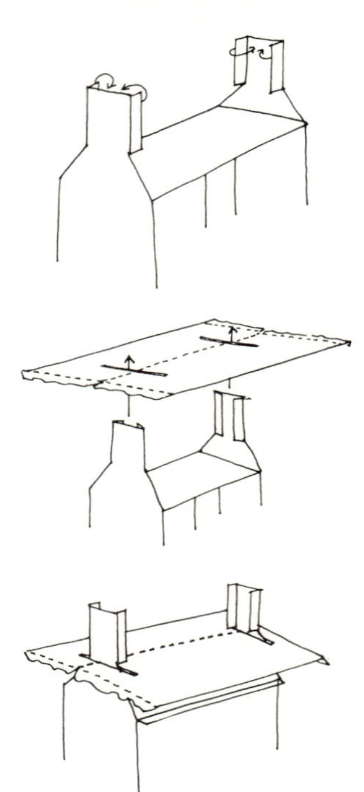

9. Fix roof to house by gluing tabs D22, A3 and A4 to spaces on underside of roof.
10. Finish by sticking down flowers and trees matching tabs to spaces.

Making the Furniture

1. Colour all the pieces using coloured pencils. Cut them out along the black lines.
2. Fold along all fold lines (if dotted, towards you; if broken, away from you).
3. Glue tabs and stick to their spaces in alphabetical order.

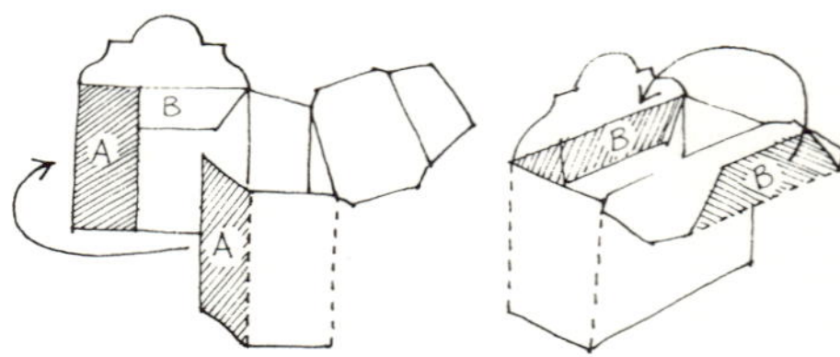

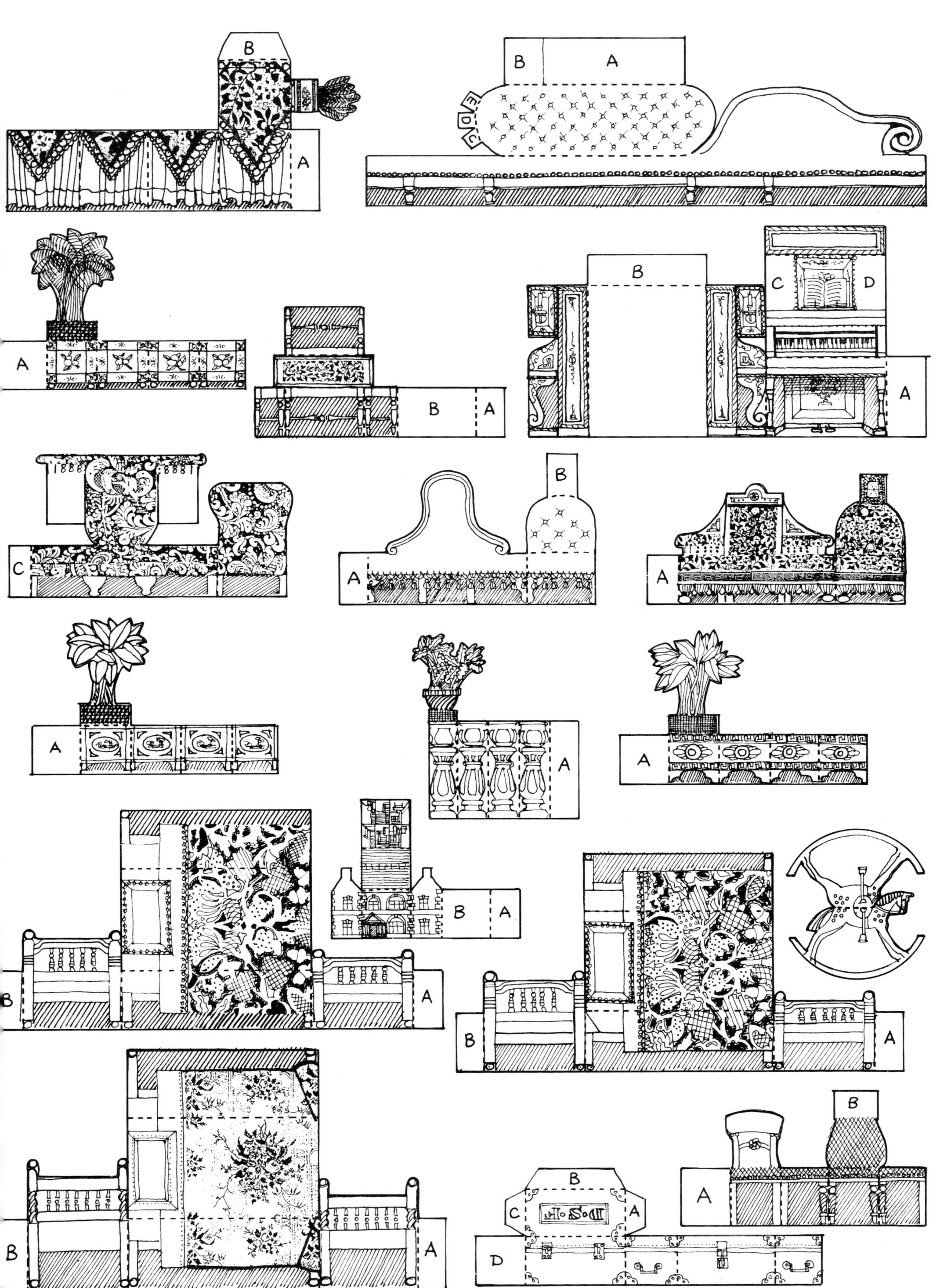

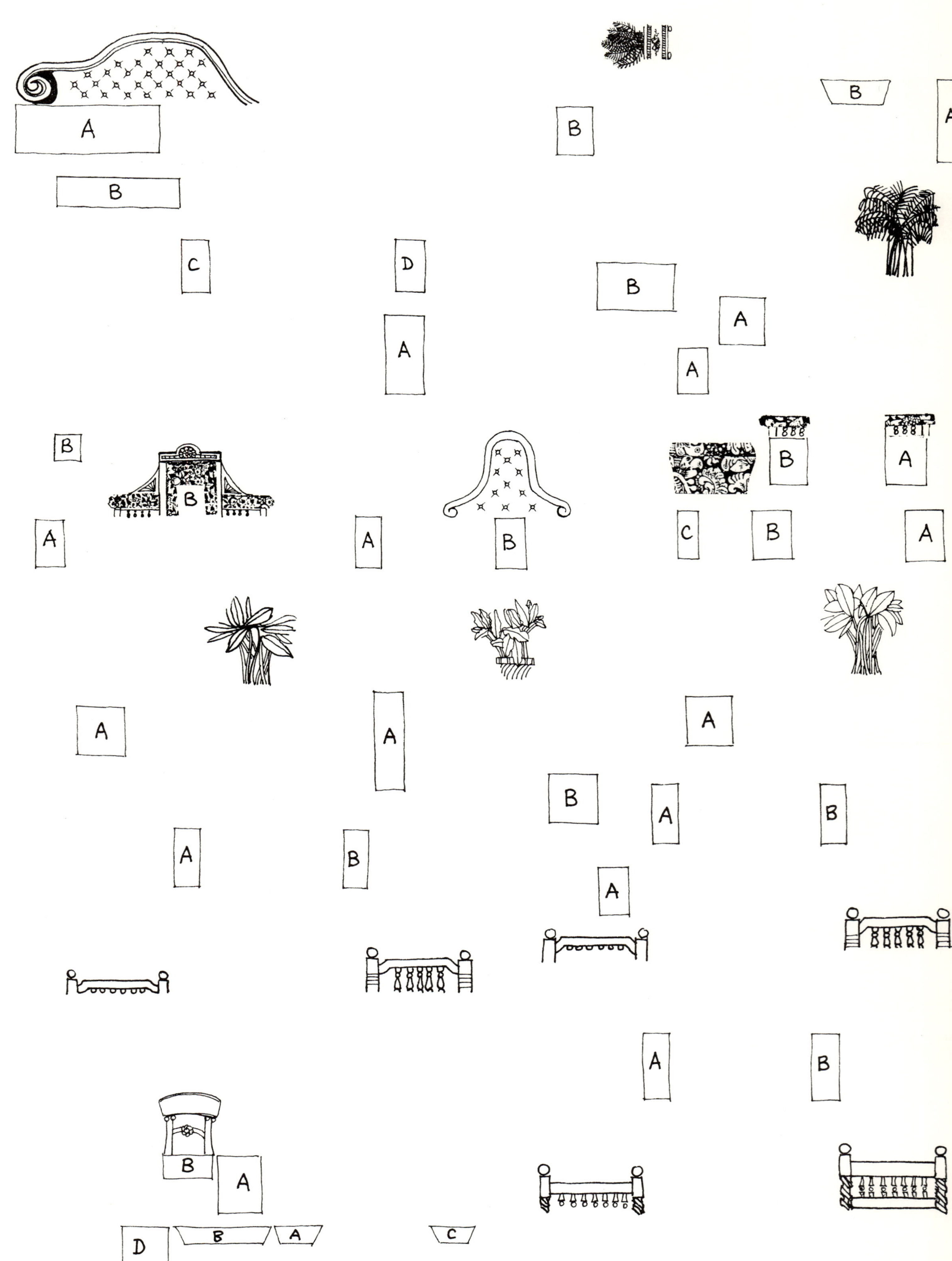
A
B
B
A
B
C
D
B
A
A
A
B
B
A
B
A
A
B
C
B
A
A
A
A
B
A
B
A
B
A
A
B
B
A
D
B
A
C

D20

BACK OF SHEET D

D5

D4

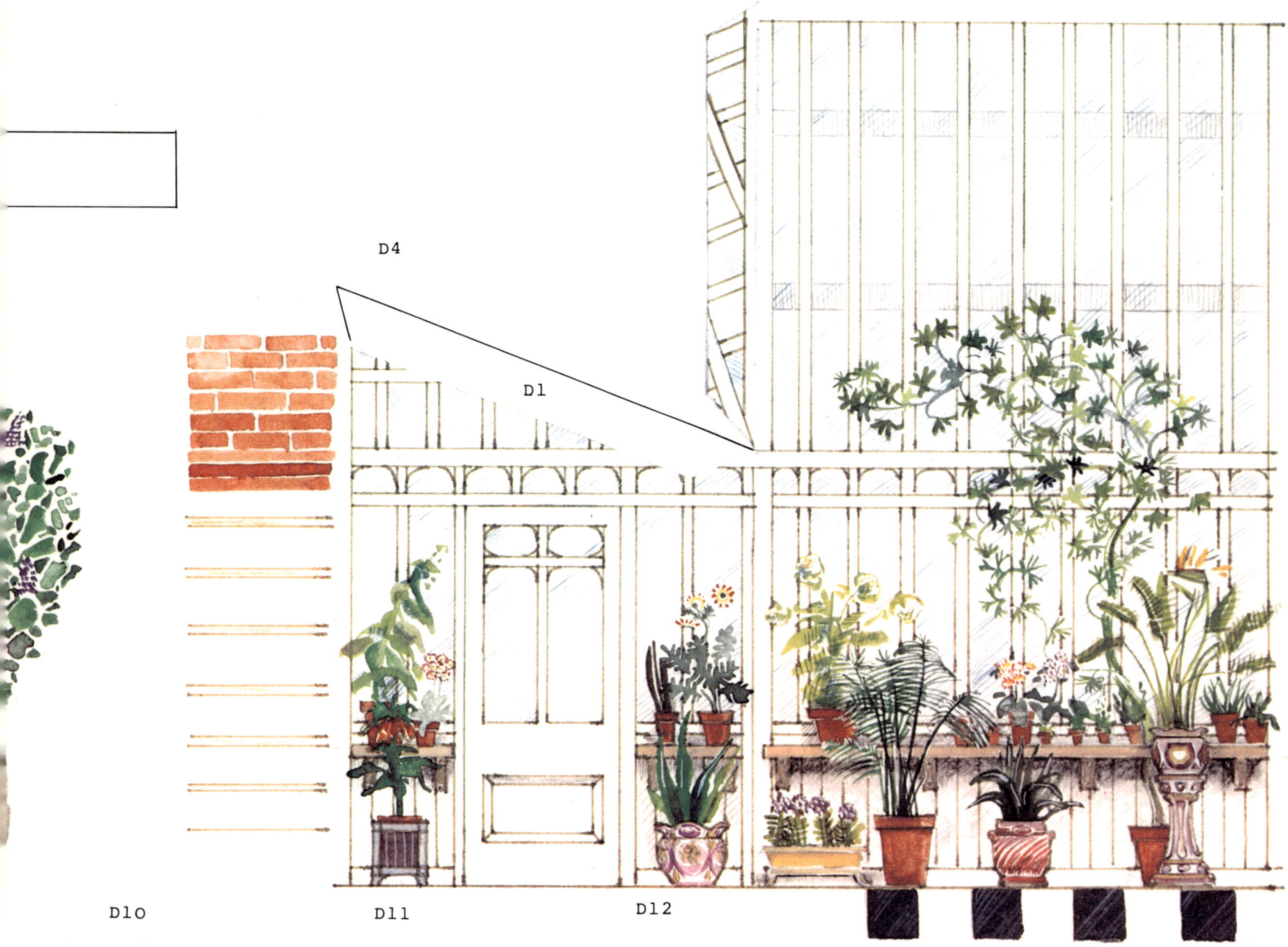

D1

D10

D11

D12

Mrs. Minns
Dolly
Tom Rawlings
George
SHEET D
D1
D17
D13

A2
D7
D14
D19
D27
A3
B5
D8
B6
D9
A4
D25
D23
D10
A5
D11
D24
D22
D12
D13
D15
D18

BACK OF STAIR WALL

B3

STICK DOWN ON TOP FLOOR LANDING

B4

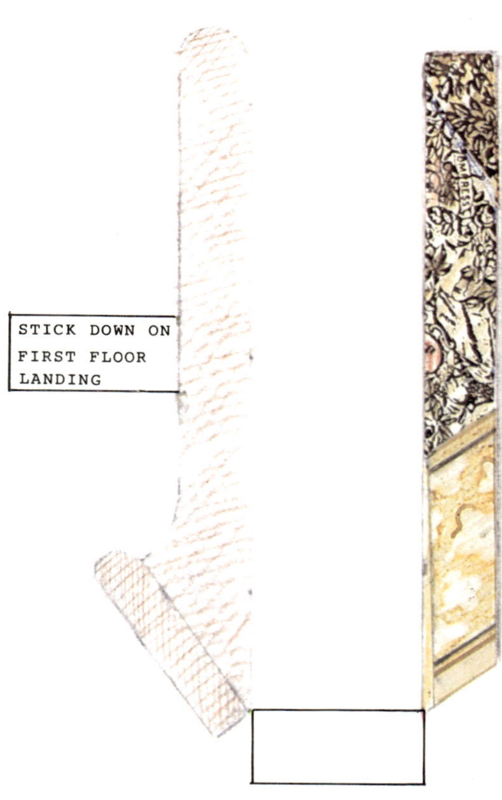

STICK DOWN ON FIRST FLOOR LANDING

BACK OF SHEET B

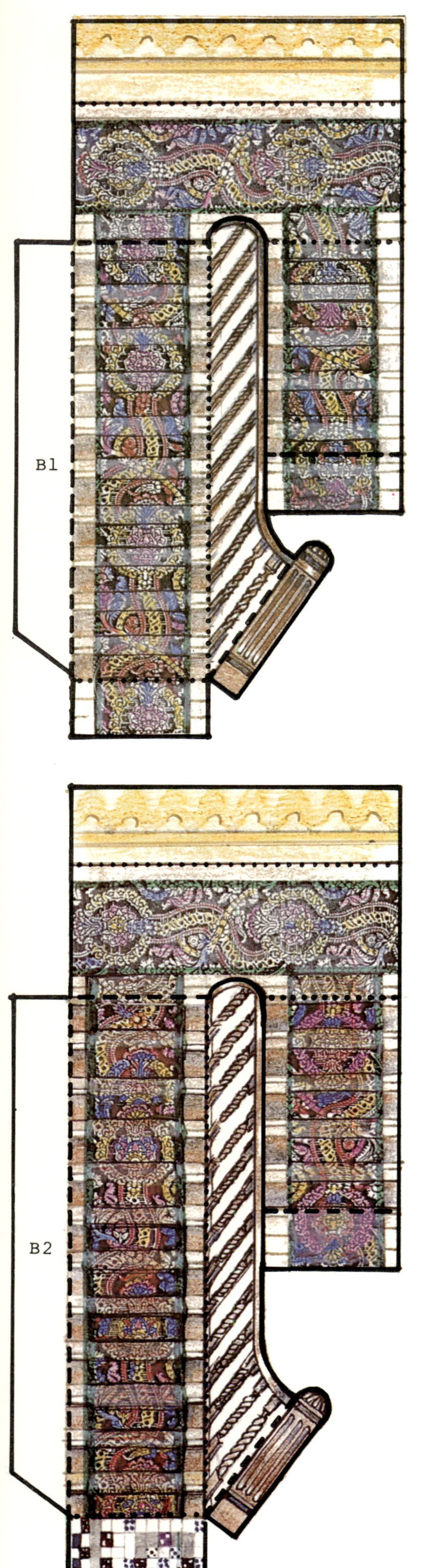

B3

B1

B4

B2

B5

D20

D21

C4

C1

C8

C5

A5

Father
Mother
Emily
Lucy
A1
A2
D6
D5
D4

D3

A4

A3

C2

C3

A1

GLUE BACK OF STAIR WALL HERE

C6

C7

A3

A4

B8
B6
B7

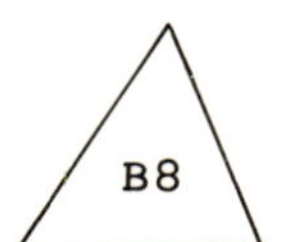

SLOT

A4

D22

A3

SLOT

B7

D17
D16
D26

SHEET C

C4
C5
C3
C6
C2
C7
C1
C8

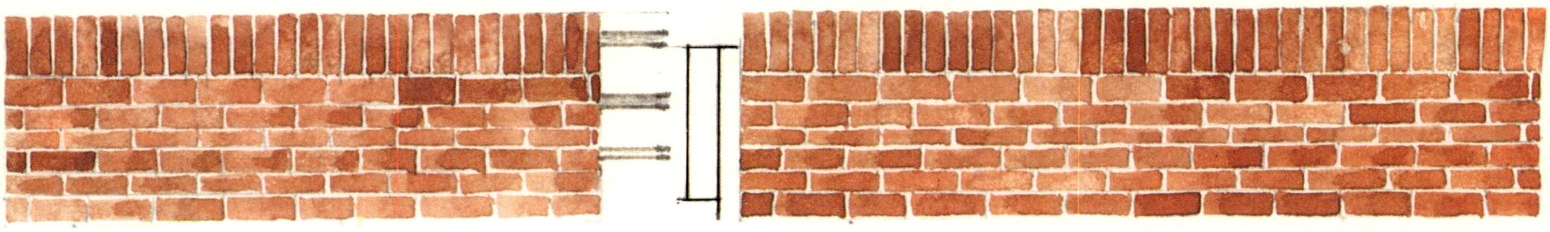

D19

D18

D14

D15

BACK OF SHEET C

D22
D24
D25
D26
D16

D21

D3

D2

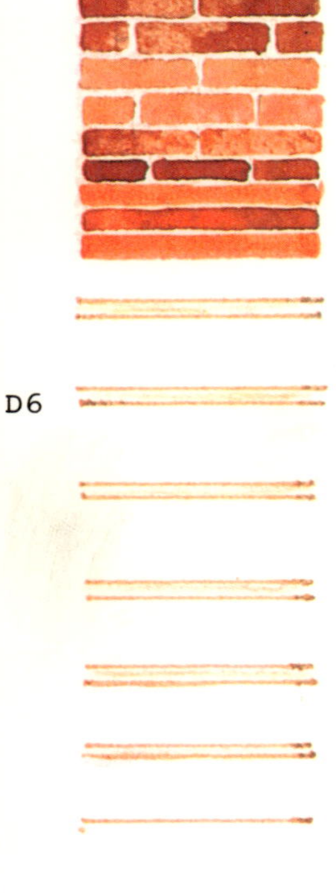

D6

D25

D24

D7

D8

D9

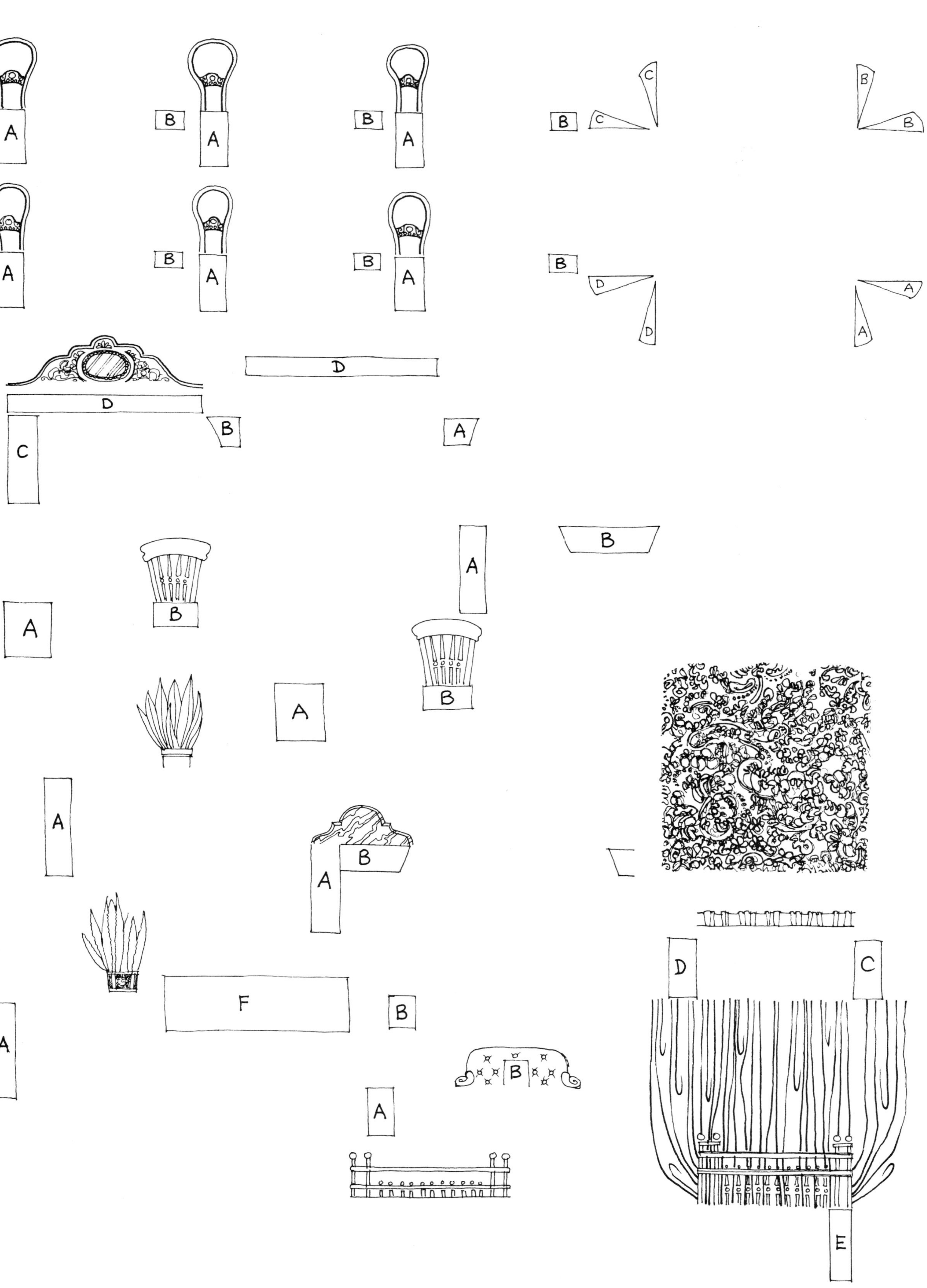

B
A
B
A
B
A
B
A
B
A
B
A
A
B
C
B
A
B
A
B
A
A
B
A
B
A
C
D
A
A
F
E

When you have made your Victorian House you can have fun acting this play, using the characters in the house.

A Jubilee Surprise

A one-act Play set in June 1887 on the day of Queen Victoria's Golden Jubilee.

Cast

Father
Mother
Their daughters: Emily aged 12
Lucy aged 8
Mrs. Minns, the housekeeper/cook
Dolly, the general maid
George, aged 10, Dolly's brother
Tom Rawlings, a delivery boy

Scene 1 — The Dining Room

It is breakfast-time and Father, Mother and the two girls are seated at the table. Father is reading his paper.

Mother: If you have quite finished, girls, I will tell Dolly that she can clear away now. Emily, you have hardly touched your bacon and kidneys! There are children starving on the other side of the Empire who would be grateful for the food you waste.

Emily: I'm sorry, Mama. I'm too excited to eat. Just think — this is Jubilee Day. The Queen has reigned for fifty years!

Mother: Emily, you are making my head spin! Please be quiet, dear.

Father: I must be off to the office!

Lucy: Oh, Father, must you really work today? Everyone should be having a holiday to celebrate the Golden Jubilee!

Father: Yes, I must, I'm afraid. Now girls, be good, and remember to do at least one good turn to someone poorer than yourself today.

Lucy and Emily: Yes, Father. Goodbye, Father.

Father: Goodbye, my dears.

He kisses his wife, and departs through the front door.

Mother: I have a headache coming on. Dolly!

Enter the maid.

Mother: You may clear. I am going to lie down this morning, in the drawing room. Go to your room, Emily and Lucy. You can get on with your sewing quietly today.

Mother goes up to the drawing room and lies down on the chaise-longue.

Emily: Come along, Lucy. We'd better go upstairs.

Lucy: I hate Mother's headache days — being quiet all the time. I wanted to go out and see the Queen today. Oh, it's not fair!

Emily: Don't scowl, Lucy. You know what Cook says — the wind might change and leave you looking cross for ever.

Lucy: I just don't feel like sewing, that's all. Let's go down to see Cook.

Scene 2 — The Kitchen

Cook and Dolly are clearing up the breakfast things. There is a knock at the door.

Cook: See who that is, Dolly.

Dolly opens the back door.

Tom: Special delivery. Special cake, ordered by your master, for the young ladies. So don't you go sticking your fingers into the icing, young Doll.

Dolly: Such cheek — as if I would! I'll report you, Tom Rawlings, and you'll lose your place.

Tom: I'm leaving anyway. Not going to be a baker's boy all my life! I'm off to join the Navy. 'Bye, Doll, goodbye, Cook.

He leaves.

Cook: It will do that young lad good, I reckon. Now put that cake away quickly, Dolly.

The door opens and Emily and Lucy run in.

Lucy: Oh, Dolly, what have you got there?

Emily: Let's see! It's a Jubilee Cake! Did Father order it? How lovely! We'll have it for tea and it will make us feel quite festive after all.

Cook: Now, Miss Emily, you've spoilt the master's surprise!

Emily: Sorry, Cook. We'll pretend it's a surprise for Father, don't worry.

Lucy: Come upstairs, Emily, and let us see if we can glimpse the crowds over at Paddington from the bedroom window.

The girls rush upstairs to their bedroom on the top floor.

Scene 3 — The Girls' Bedroom

Emily: I wish the boys were here instead of at boarding school.

Lucy: I don't — they'd eat all the cake! Can you see anything out of that window? The Queen will be arriving at Paddington on her way to Buckingham Palace from Windsor any minute now.

Emily: No — but I can hear the crowds! Listen!

Emily pulls a chair over to the window and climbs up.

Lucy: I want to see, too. I know, I'll get the chair from Dolly's room.

Lucy goes across the landing to Dolly's room.

Scene 4 — Dolly's Bedroom

Lucy picks up a chair. As she turns back to the door she sees a boy hiding behind it.

Lucy: Oh! Who are you?

George: I'm not doing anything wrong, miss. I promise.

Enter Emily.

Emily: Who are you talking to, Lucy? Oh . . . Who is this? Was he trying to steal something?

George: 'Course I wasn't. Our Doll said it'd be all right to stay here. You just ask 'er.

Enter Dolly.

Dolly: Oh lor! George!

Emily: Do you know this boy, Dolly?

Dolly: 'Course I do, Miss Emily. It's my youngest brother, George. Oh, please don't turn us out on the streets, miss! I never meant any 'arm!

Emily: Maybe this is our chance to do the good turn to someone poorer than ourselves that Father mentioned, Lucy. Now, Dolly, tell us all about it.

Dolly: I'm an orphan, miss. Like George here. And our brother Will. All the rest of our family was taken in the cholera a couple of years ago. That's when I'd just started work here.

George: And Will got a job scaring birds for fourpence a day. Kept us fine, that did.

Dolly: But Will got caught with a sheepskin he was using as a blanket, and the farmer accused him of stealing it. So now he's being sent to prison, and George has come looking for me. What'll I do, Miss Emily?

Lucy: Let's hide him in our room.

Emily: We can't do that. We must tell Mother.

Dolly: Oh, don't do that, please, Miss Emily!

George: I'm off!

George dives out of the room and down the stairs to first floor landing and creeps into the drawing room.

Emily: Quick! After him!

The girls rush downstairs, followed by Dolly. On the landing they collide with Cook, who is coming up from the kitchen.

Scene 5 — The Drawing Room

Mother: (*waking up at the noise*) What is going on? Oh! An urchin!

George: I'm not an urchin! I'm a visitor!

Mother: (*panicking*) Cook! Cook, where are you?

Enter Cook.

Cook: Yes, madam.

Mother: Cook, show this urchin the door, at once!

Enter Emily and Lucy.

Emily: Can't we help him, Mother? It's Dolly's brother.

Mother: What can I possibly do for him? All right — give this ragamuffin something to eat before you show him out, Cook.

Cook, Dolly and George go down to the kitchen.

Enter Father.

Father: Hello, my dears? It was such a lovely day that I settled the urgent business and left the rest for another day. So the cake came! I met the baker's lad — he's off to join the Navy!

Emily: It's a lovely cake, Father. Thank you. I must tell you about Dolly's brother. . . .

Father: The baker will be sorry to lose him, I fear. The lad lived in like one of the family, I believe. Always cheerful. I'll miss seeing him around. I should think he'll make a good sailor.

Emily: Oh, Father, can't we do something to help Dolly's brother. He's got nowhere to go. . . .

Father: What's all this about Dolly's brother? I didn't even know she had a brother.

Emily: He's down in the kitchen with Cook. He hasn't got a job or a home, and. . . .

Father: Wait a minute! I've had an idea. Let's go down and take a look at the lad.

Scene 6 — The Kitchen

Cook is showing George to the door. Dolly stands by looking miserable.

Cook: I don't care who you are, you can't stay here. You heard the mistress.

Dolly: Boo hoo!

Enter Father, Mother and the girls.

Father: Wait!

Cook stops.

Father: Come with me, boy. You and I are going on a short visit down the road.

George: Not the law! Oh, don't turn me in, Sir, I haven't pinched anything!

Dolly: Have mercy, Sir! Have pity!

Father: Quiet, both of you. Nothing was farther from my mind. We are going to pay a visit to the baker, George. I happen to know he is in need of a delivery boy and I think you would be admirably suited.

George: What about that, Doll? Thank you, Sir.

Father: When I get back we'll take a Hackney cab to view the Queen's arrival at Buckingham Palace.

Mother: Quickly, girls, go and tidy yourselves. Dolly, fetch my parasol, if you please!

Dolly: Oh, Ma'am! With pleasure! Thank you, Sir — I'll never forget the Queen's Golden Jubilee.

THE END.